To read fluently is one of the basic aims of anyone learning English as a foreign language. **And it's never too early to start**. Ladybird Graded Readers are interesting but simple stories designed to encourage children between the ages of 6 and 10 to read with pleasure.

Reading is an excellent way of reinforcing language already acquired, as well as broadening a child's vocabulary. Ladybird Graded Readers use a limited number of grammatical structures and a carefully controlled vocabulary, but where the story demands it, a small number of words outside the basic vocabulary are introduced. In *Gingerbread Man* the following words are outside the basic vocabulary for this grade:

back, fox, gingerbread man, oven, tail

Further details of the structures and vocabulary used at each grade can be found in the Ladybird Graded Readers leaflet.

A list of books in the series can be found on the back cover.

British Library Cataloguing in Publication Data
Ullstein, Sue
  Gingerbread man.
  I. Title   II. Price Thomas, Brian
  428.6'4
  ISBN 0-7214-1215-7

First edition
Published by Ladybird Books Ltd Loughborough Leicestershire UK
Ladybird Books Inc Auburn Maine 04210 USA
© LADYBIRD BOOKS LTD MCMLXXXIX
Printed in England

Gingerbread Man

written by Sue Ullstein
illustrated by Brian Price Thomas

Ladybird Books

An old man and an old woman live on a farm.

Two children come to the farm.
They want to help the old
man and the old woman.

The old woman says,
"Let's make some good things
for supper. Do you want
a gingerbread man?"

"Yes, please," the children say.
"We like gingerbread.
Let's make a gingerbread man."

They make a gingerbread man.

The old woman puts
the gingerbread man
into the oven.

When she takes the
gingerbread man out of
the oven, she says,
''This is a good gingerbread
man! We'll eat him for
supper.''

The gingerbread man looks at the old woman.

"No, no," he says.
"You can't eat me!
No one can eat me!"

He jumps off the table.
And he runs away.

"Stop, stop!" the old woman shouts.

"No, I won't stop," the gingerbread man says.
"You can't catch me!"

And he runs out of the house.

The old man sees the
gingerbread man.

"Stop, gingerbread man!"
he shouts. "The children
want to eat you for supper."

"No, no," the gingerbread man says. "I won't stop.
The old woman can't catch me and you can't catch me. No one can eat me for supper!"

And he runs on.

The children see
the gingerbread man.

''Stop, gingerbread man!''
they shout. ''We want to eat you
for supper.''

"No, no," the gingerbread man says. "I won't stop.
The old woman can't catch me.
The old man can't catch me and you can't catch me. No one can eat me for supper!"

And he runs on.

A horse sees
the gingerbread man.

"Stop, gingerbread man!"
he says. "I want to eat you
for supper."

"No, no," the gingerbread man says. "I won't stop.
The old woman can't catch me.
The old man can't catch me.
The children can't catch me
and you can't catch me. No one
can eat me for supper!"

And he runs on.

A cow sees the gingerbread man.

''Stop, gingerbread man!''
she says. ''I want to eat you
for supper.''

"No, no," the gingerbread man says. "I won't stop.
The old woman can't catch me.
The old man can't catch me.
The children can't catch me.
The horse can't catch me
and you can't catch me. No one can eat me for supper!"

And he runs on.

A dog sees the gingerbread man.

''Stop, gingerbread man!''
he says. ''I want to eat you
for supper.''

"No, no," the gingerbread man says. "I won't stop.
The old woman can't catch me.
The old man can't catch me.
The children can't catch me.
The horse can't catch me.
The cow can't catch me
and you can't catch me. No one can eat me for supper."

And he runs on.

A cat sees the gingerbread man.

"Stop, gingerbread man,"
she says. "I want to eat you
for supper."

"No, no," the gingerbread man says. "I won't stop.
The old woman can't catch me.
The old man can't catch me.
The children can't catch me.
The horse can't catch me.
The cow can't catch me.
The dog can't catch me
and you can't catch me. No one can eat me for supper."

And he runs on.

The gingerbread man comes
to a river.

"What can I do?" he says.
"I must get across the river,
but I can't swim. The cat
and the dog and the cow
and the horse and the children
and the old man
and the old woman
all want to eat me.
I must get across
the river."

The gingerbread man
sees a fox.

"Let me help you," the fox
says. "I can swim.
Sit on my tail."

"Thank you, Mr Fox,"
the gingerbread man says.

He jumps onto the fox's tail.
The fox goes into the river.

Soon the gingerbread man's feet
are in the water.

"Help me, Mr Fox,"
the gingerbread man says.
"My feet are in the water."

"Then jump onto my back,"
the fox says.

The gingerbread man
jumps onto the fox's back.

The fox swims on.

44

Soon the gingerbread man's feet
are in the water again.

"Help me, Mr Fox,"
the gingerbread man says.
"My feet are in the water again."

"Then jump onto my head,"
the fox says.

The gingerbread man jumps
onto the fox's head.

The fox swims on.

Soon the gingerbread man's feet
are in the water again.

"Help me, Mr Fox,"
the gingerbread man says.
"My feet are in the water again."

"Then jump onto my nose,"
the fox says.

The gingerbread man jumps
onto the fox's nose.

Then SNAP!

The fox eats
the gingerbread man!

So, there was no gingerbread man
for the cat or the dog
or the cow or the horse

or the children or the old man
or the old woman.
And they all went home again.